AWARE

A Guide for Christian Families in an LGBTQ Culture

The Purpose of AWARE

The purpose of this booklet is to bring an awareness of the current social, educational, and spiritual situation regarding SSA (same sex attraction) and homosexuality to parents and families. This guide will serve to assist parents in putting SSA and homosexuality into a historical and biblical context, dispel some popular myths, reframe the issue into a Christian worldview, and give parents resources and places to go that are seldom if ever mentioned or highlighted in the popular cultural debate. Aware is not intended to be a comprehensive study of the subject of sexual orientation. Use it as a conversation starter with your teenagers – a simple guide to be used wisely in conjunction with other Christian parental resources.

How Did We Get Here?

The cultural climate in the United States has dramatically changed in the past decade regarding many issues confronting the Christian faith - none of these more so than the issue of sexual orientation and homosexuality. In many ways the LGBTQ (lesbian, gay, bisexual, transgendered, Questioning) community and its partners have put themselves at the forefront of the social curve influencing adults through entertainment and media and also our children through educational programs within public schools. Most parents of faith find that they need help putting it all into a proper Christian context as well as communicating the truth in love to their children – who face a very non-Christian worldview everyday. Like it or not we are truly parenting in an LGBTQ culture.

What does it mean to come out as gay?

To most of the secular (non-Christian) culture, coming out as gay means that a man or woman has finally come to grips with who they are; that after much struggle and trial, they are finally claiming their true identity once and for all. For most people who develop SSA, they have had feelings of attraction toward the same sex for years before they finally let others know. It is not uncommon that this struggle with identity leads to anxiety, depression, and a sense of loneliness or isolation. Suicide rates are higher for young gay men than others[1]. Many fight this early sense of attraction to the same sex and strongly desire heterosexual feelings. They will date and even marry in an attempt to live heterosexually. For many though, the SSA does not go away and they feel as if they're living a lie. In coming out, there is a huge sense of release that this hidden secret is now in the open and they can truly be what they assume they were born to be – gay.

It's important for Christians to remember that while coming out is a sense of relief for the individual, it does nothing to address the root issues that led to the formation of SSA in the first place. In fact, there are few if any broad social-psychological services that deal with the conflicting traumas resulting in SSA. The gay-identified individual is then left with the initial life-struggle as well as the symptom (SSA) while being told that accepting and even celebrating this symptom is the ultimate answer to their internal conflict. Is it any wonder then that the gay population, even in accepting and loving environments, commits suicide at rates higher than the general population? Symptom celebrating is no panacea from internal conflict.

What Does Science Say About Sexual Orientation?

In such an important conversation, it's important that we understand the science of the issue. If we look at sexual orientation from a just-the-facts scenario, what do we see? Let's bullet point the highlights:

- Approximately 3% to 4% of the adult population identifies as gay[2].
- The myth of the gay gene has been busted. It's not as simple as someone being born gay.[3] Although biology and genetics may certainly play a role, the size and scope of the orientation hardwiring is seemingly smaller than was first thought and only one factor among many.
- Environmental factors seem to play a large in determining the development of SSA. These factors include things such as physical, sexual, and / or emotional abuse at an early age. The inability to attach pre-puberty to their father in a healthy way, a sense of abandonment or detachment from the father, and a real (or even perceived) inability to please or live up to the father's expectations.[4]
- Development of SSA seems to be a complex mixture of personality and temperament + environment + genetics and evolves developmentally during pre-puberty.
- Those who struggle with SSA didn't choose it overtly. It seems to have chosen them. Most would choose heterosexual orientation.
- The longer the wait to identify as gay or lesbian, the greater the chance that later in life, the SSA subsides[5]

It's interesting to note that there is not much continuing research on the development of orientation and SSA. The prevailing attitude in the psychological / educational community is that homosexuality is a normal expression of human sexuality, which has always existed in historical culture. Therefore, the need to know how and why it develops is not immediate or pressing.

What part do public schools and higher education play?

Public schools and educational systems normally stress the idea of coming to grips with who you are and not suppressing your sexual orientation. School counselors are trained to accept and not judge, to generally lead and support the student as they find their way in accepting their same sex orientation. In other words, like most of the larger academic and higher educational institutions, public education is symptom driven – focusing on relief through acceptance. Most public middle and high schools will have active chapters of student run groups and clubs that give a sense of community to gay-identified individuals. The prevailing idea is one of building acceptance while normalizing their SSA - through dialogue with others. For many young people these groups are cathartic, allowing an emotional and therapeutic release of pent up feelings.

Your teenager is doing life in the midst of this learning environment. The sense of morality stressed to them in this setting is the morality of acceptance. Anything other can seem bigoted and ignorant. Of course not all schools are the same and not every environment is the same but acceptance and normalcy are the goals when it comes to school programs aimed at helping the gay-identified student. Having open and honest communication with your kids about what's being taught as well as a biblical worldview of God as loving, kind, and knowing what's best for us as His creation is a helpful start.

What does psychology say?

Much like public schools, nearly all of the secular (non-Christian) psychological counseling that gay men and women receive is geared toward acceptance of who they are. We must understand that much of the secular counseling world treats individuals with a client-centered approach that allows the counselee to set the goals and desired outcomes for treatment. The counselor cannot introduce values and judgments (or appeal to scripture) outside of what the client brings with them. Since the APA's (American Psychological Association) official stance is that homosexuality is a normal expression of human sexuality, there is no need to change orientation. Despite the fact there is evidence (both anecdotal and otherwise) that orientation in both gays and transgendered people can (for some), be fluid and changing, the official stance of the APA is that change-orientation is almost always harmful and ineffective[6]. Further, the stance from the top of the APA is often demeaning and aggressive toward those who would attempt to deal with the root issues leading to SSA and transgendered outcomes. In some states it is against the law for licensed counselors to attempt therapeutic change in the sexual orientation of a minor – even if the parents and the minor both strongly desire change[7]. It is abundantly clear that the prevailing narrative of normalcy, acceptance, and even celebration of a non-heterosexual orientation is something that is firmly rooted and widely accepted in our educational and psychological systems. Until 1973 the issue of homosexuality in individuals was listed in the DSM (the statistical manual of mental disorders) as a mental disorder. Why is it no longer considered an aberration? Just as gay identified people serve on boards and as CEOs of corporations, they have also served on the board and as past presidents of the APA. This could quite possibly effect the interpretations of gathered data and set the normalcy tone we see today. Although science itself is not subject to bias – its interpreters most certainly are.

What does scripture say – and how should we respond?

If we call ourselves Christians we must be aware of and concerned with a biblical worldview. Cultural whims cannot rule the day or set the parameters for how we view societal issues – especially this one. With that in mind, there are several mistakes that are prevalent and obvious when Christians and the church respond to the issue of homosexuality and the gay identified congregant.

There was a time not long ago when the church (depending heavily on the region of the country) would respond in an almost militant fashion to any individual seeking help and understanding with SSA. The person would hear stories about Sodom and Gomorrah along with a booklet on AIDS. Feigning a heartfelt welcome, the assumption in these churches would be that a true Christian could not struggle with such things – that this reprobate mind had been obviously given over to Satan himself. Therefore the approach would always be evangelical. If the person would truly give their heart to the Lord, God would "take the gay away." Other churches sought the exact opposite approach where gay identified congregants would be affirmed, appreciated, celebrated, and treated as special because of their sexual identity. These symptom-celebrating churches relied heavily on liberation theology and focused on relief from oppression. Overlooking the deliverance from sin through Jesus, this brand of church prefers instead deliverance from perceived societal and political oppression. In other words, the problem is with everyone else, thus offering no hope for change in the person.

These particular church strategies still exist and are carried out every day across America. Fortunately, many churches have centralized their beliefs and approach of the issue, learning from mistakes of the past. Most have a very genuine love and compassion for strugglers of all kinds, including SSA, and do a good job ministering truth in love to hurting people. This is how we should strive to respond.

In light of these things, scripture is still clear that homosexuality is sin. To be clear, the embracing of a lifestyle that acts upon one's SSA and creates an environment of normalcy for it is wrong - in the same way it would be wrong to normalize any other sin. We are to die to the flesh, not normalize it. The following is a list of primary scriptures in the New Testament that deals with homosexuality in its proper context:

- <u>Matthew 19:1-8</u> – Jesus issues a sweeping condemnation of sexual relationships outside of the male-female marriage model.

- <u>Romans 1:18-32</u> – For the first time female homosexuality is mentioned and attributed in a wider way to the depravity of humanity (due to the fall in Genesis 3).
- <u>1 Corinthians 6:9-11</u> – Probably the most explicit of the N.T. verses. Paul acknowledges that some of his reading audience at Corinth would have been former homosexuals. Paul's tone gives tremendous hope for those who desire to change.
- <u>Galatians 5:19</u> – Many areas in which Paul traveled were accepting and celebratory of homosexuals. Paul's emphasis continued to be on the works of the flesh vs. being filled with the Spirit.
- <u>Ephesians 5:3-7, Colossians 3:5-7</u> – Other passages from Paul dealing with existing troubles within the churches including homosexuality and temple prostitution.

It's important in our ever evolving (devolving?) culture that we teach this standard and don't lower the bar, so to speak, especially with our kids. Knowing that God has a divine plan that male-female relationships and sexual intimacy are to be found in the safety and sanctity of marriage is the bottom line. Cultural whims come and go but God's truth is eternal. Knowing the truth is great; beating people up with it is not.

My teenager says they are gay or trans – what now?
Don't panic and don't overreact. Don't treat this as a death sentence for your teenager. It's certainly not. One of the very first things to keep in mind is how difficult telling you (or someone else) has probably been

for them. Those struggling with orientation issues generally have a hard time admitting it and an even harder time telling someone. Admitting they have those feelings is a big first step. Applaud them for that. Denial is gone and you can now establish open and honest communication on their level. Below are some things to strive for as you go through this journey:

- Don't define their entire existence by their orientation. They are far more than their spiritual and physical struggles. Continue to communicate about all of the other important issues in their life.
- Remind yourself (and your teen) often that orientation struggle is not a sin – acting upon it is. They didn't ask to be attracted to the same sex or feel trapped in the wrong body. They didn't choose to feel this way. Their struggles are rooted in the same thing as your struggles (Genesis 3, Romans 7:21)
- Keep open and safe communication with them that stresses your unconditional love as a parent. Be patient. Remember, how they feel is how they feel, and there will be ups and downs all along the way. Rejoice in the good days and be prepared for the others.
- Make Jesus the emphasis, not their struggle. Your main goal and purpose is not to remove every ounce of their orientation issues, (that may never happen). Your main goal is that they grow in Christ and have a strong relationship with Him. As they do, God gets bigger and their struggle gets more manageable.
- Don't push your son to get a girlfriend (or your daughter to get a boyfriend), that's not a cure. If your son is questioning his gender,

don't buy him an off-road pickup truck. Instead, get counseling from a Christian source that can deal with root issues. Understanding (or attempting to) the development of SSA or other orientation issues can be very healing. For some this is a crucial and necessary step in advancing a more heterosexual leaning and orientation. For others, who may never change, it's simply a needed therapeutic release that gives greater understanding to their ongoing struggle.

- Discuss with them that our identity is never in our sexuality. We belong to Christ and our identity is in Him (Ephesians 1). Emphasize in safe communication that we never label ourselves as gay, bisexual, lesbian, trans, or anything else. We are simply followers of Christ. We have been adopted and defined by Him, not a cultural label.

- Although you may wear many hats as a parent, you are shepherding their heart through this struggle. Love them wisely while nurturing your relationship. They may become depressed, anxious, and want to isolate at times so be prepared to initiate conversation and plan time together.

- Please don't beat yourself up as a parent because your child struggles. Your parenting may or may not have had a direct effect on your teen's development in this area. It could be their perception of the environment at home and not the reality that bears the most weight. As parents, remember that on this side of heaven, struggles with personal issues will be the norm for us all. We're not home yet so allow yourself some grace.

My gay or trans teenager doesn't want to change

Please keep in mind that teens will respond to orientation issues in different ways. While some may actively fight against the attraction to others of the same sex (or the desire to be the opposite sex) and seek help on a spiritual level to deal with it, not all will. There is no guarantee that your child will see wrong in it and seek to get help. Beyond trying to please you they may not see the big deal in being gay or trans. Despite the activist's cries of oppression, the pull of society is pretty much one way in this discussion. Your teen may have already sought out a caring and empathetic community of likeminded people who don't share your values or your brand of Christian faith. So, what can a parent do if their child chooses to identify anyway?

- Once again, don't minimize their entire existence to the size of this issue. They are more than their sexual orientation so your conversations should entail more as well.

- Love them more and need them less.[8] Search your heart (Psalm 139) and make certain that you aren't reacting to this issue in unhealthy neediness. I *need them* to be straight so they don't embarrass me, so they authenticate me, so my parenting life would not have been a failure, etc. If your identity (and value) is caught up in their identity you may have an even more difficult journey ahead. It's not your responsibility to have Godly children. It's your responsibility to make sure your children have Godly parents. There will always be an ebb and flow to their journey before God.

- Never give up spiritually. Continually intercede in prayer for them just as you would if they were caught up in any other stronghold.

- Your teen may request to date others of the same sex or have a friend over that they're interested in. They may have a strong desire to dress as the opposite sex and wear things that might embarrass you. Please remember, you have the right (and responsibility) to set boundaries in your home and enforce them. The attraction isn't sin; confusion about your gender isn't sin. Acting on it is.

- It would be good for you and your teenager to go to Christian counseling and learn how to communicate, set boundaries, respect and love each other through this. Nearly every relationship will go through seasons of competing agendas. Learning how to negotiate through them in ways that value what's eternal and offer respect and love to each person is huge. Have hope - your relationship can make it through this season.

How do I talk to my kids about their friends who struggle?

It's important to remind your kids that we live in a world that is not as it was first created. We live in a fallen world (Genesis 3). Bible studies and family devotions are great conversation starters and help to weave what they see and hear from culture through a biblical worldview. Allowing your kids to see their parents' willingness to take time to read and pray with them has many immeasurable benefits as well. Your local church youth and student groups should also be places where there are healthy, honest conversations and teaching aimed at maturing your teenager in their faith and view of the world. These are typically safe places to ask questions and voice opinions while learning God's truth.

One of the most important conversations to have with your teens regarding the issue of SSA / transgender is that of seeing us how God sees us – that we are fallen and in need of rescue. That while these things are a struggle for some, God loves strugglers – and so should we. We are not the judge and the jury. Our job is to love God and love people. Jesus wouldn't avoid, dismiss, or relegate anyone to second-class-citizen status and neither should we. So talk to your teens about their gay friends or those they know that are actively struggling. How do they view them? How do they pray for them? This is the stuff of ministry.

On the other hand, it may be that your teens (especially older ones) don't see these issues the same way as you do. They may not see an issue with it at all. The fact that kids and parents disagree is not new and they may already have close friends and family who have come out. These things along with the fact that nearly every movie, sitcom, or reality show involves gay characters means that we are heavily familiarized with the Hollywood version of what it means to be gay. And just as this media-driven desensitization has affected the adult general populace, it has influenced the young as well. Most people are shocked that the actual percentage of gay identified (and transgendered) people in America is such a small percentage of the population given the overwhelming presence presented in film and popular media. Again, another talking point for you and your kids as you work through the cultural whims of our day and the weighty pull that they have on us.

Be reminded (and encouraged) that we're certainly not the first or the last Christians to swim against the tide of popular opinion in a cultural setting - far from it. Incredibly, nearly everywhere Paul planted churches the populace would have been open and accepting of sexually extreme lifestyles. It was a world where worship of God was inherently and vilely mixed with worship of sexual desires of all sorts. The Greco-Roman culture with its famous bathhouses, temple prostitutes, and pagan priests would have presented early believers with an incredible challenge to be both loving and truthful. How did Paul address these issues? How did he encourage the early believers to keep themselves from these things and yet be salt and light in the world?

Finally, it's always good when talking with your teens about their friends who are same sex attracted or gender confused, to keep the conversation in the context of our struggles. These things are not outside the realm of normal human struggle. Paul says in Romans that there is a law that evil is present in me, the one who wants to do good (Romans 7:21). Every human struggles with something, so what do we do with ours? All of these and more are fruitful, continual talking points to have with your teens.

Should my teenager have gay or transgendered friends?

For some parents this question will be difficult. Many feel that a gay or transgendered lifestyle is wrong and while they know their child can't live in a bubble, the strong exposure of friendship is worrisome for some parents. Could camaraderie with those who are out and open influence your child to act out? Can having openly gay friends sway your teen into unwanted SSA? Could having pizza with a transgendered classmate cause your son or daughter to question their gender? The answer to each is - probably not - especially if your child is one of the 96% - 97% of people that are heterosexual. There just isn't evidence to suggest that having gay or trans friends can alter sexual orientation. In reality, many types of friends will influence your teen and drawing a circle around just one in particular may not be the best approach. So, unless they are crossing boundaries and being an unhealthy friend, the best approach may not be to prohibit the friendship based on their orientation. The best approach may be to communicate openly with your child concerning the friend and what's going on their life. In doing so, listen to the heart behind the words of your teenager. How do they view their friend? What does being a genuine friend look like? Have they talked to their friend about Jesus or invited them to church? How do they pray for them? Remember, while parenting involves many things, you are at the core, a shepherd. You are shepherding your teen's heart as they navigate through the minefields of a fallen world. Openness, honesty, and communicating well will pay bigger dividends with your child than boundaries that may be based too much in personal bias or unwarranted fear.

That aside, the final decision is yours as a parent and should be made with much prayer and wisdom. *We must love people wisely*, especially those struggling with orientation and sexual sin. The amount of time your child spends with a gay or transgendered friend may need to be limited and their focus (of being Christ-like) needs to be in the forefront. It would be easy for your teenager to be caught up in the activism of the day and the progressive gender-bender struggle that has saturated our media and academic culture. Your teen's natural and God-given instinct to be more gradually independent of parental oversight can easily be hijacked by these not-so-friendly, almost militant agendas whose talking points can prove powerful to the undeveloped discernment of the young. Balance in these matters and open communication with your teen is the key. No one said this parenting thing would be easy!

Final thoughts

Sexual sins are many times indicators of deeper emotional needs that we are attempting to meet in all the wrong ways[9]. SSA and transgenderism are prime examples. The young man who is a wonderfully creative, sensitive, soul but is damaged by an angry, abusive father; the young girl marred by molestation who then endures years of bullying in school, these along with dozens of other tragic scenarios are played out thousands of times in the lives of young people - all of whom are coping with their tragic narrative in various ways. And for a select few, this coping strategy will be chosen for them fairly young via their traumatically influenced biochemistry. SSA and (to some extent) transgenderism, is their body's auto-response to the emotional damage they've encountered. Like most coping skills they don't work well but to some clunky degree they do work. As inherently deficient as these are at addressing root issues in meaningful ways, they *seem* to bring a sense of relief – albeit fleeting, shallow, and temporary.

Our culture, like many worldwide, has embraced theses symptoms, these coping mechanisms, and have normalized and celebrated their existence, making it all the more difficult to find a reason to change. No change needed, no change sought. In effect, through this cultural normalization we have resigned people to an existence of personal identity through sexual sin. In this brave new world, their orientation sets the agenda for everything else – it has to. After all, it's their orientation that is handling the weight of their inner struggle attempting to somehow right the emotional, psychological, and even physical wounds that they've experienced. It's an automated course correction that they didn't overtly choose. This correction, however, is fatally flawed from the beginning. It leads the struggler to search for rescue where it can never be found – in the creation (in us or in others) rather than the Creator. In self, as the transgendered finds hope in finally becoming the gender they feel they were really meant to be, or in others as the person with SSA finds love where they were never meant to find it. The journey is a long and frustrating one as ultimate help and hope is never found outside of God. How do we respond?

These strugglers deserve our support, love, encouragement, and faithful friendship - not our judgment and wrath. Why? As Christ followers we are not called to be passive and enabling. Our support and love should show up vibrantly by stepping into the difficult and often confusing world of the LGBTQ community when called upon to do so – especially when it comes to our kids. Scripture is overflowing with painful, real, and oftentimes grotesque pictures of human sin and its consequences. The deep nature of sin is a well-documented theme throughout. Divine beauty occurs when our ever-faithful God shows His relentless pursuit of the fallen and offers rescue. We see the measure of

His compassion on the cross and His limitless power in the resurrection. This is the God we cling to in times such as these. He loves and plans for our kids more than we ever could. So we are to be active in the way we support, love, and encourage strugglers.[10] Amen.

Finally, we must remember that this is a uniquely free country in which we live. America is blessed and beautiful but she's not eternal. Our more conservative nature has given way from tolerance to acceptance to normalization (and even celebration) of many things that were considered taboo and sinful just a few short decades ago. Historically, that pendulum rarely swings back the other way. Once a culture progresses (some would say regresses) values-wise in its core principles, the things-that-were are simply gone. It's very legal in the United Sates for men to marry men and women to marry women, for gay and lesbian couples to adopt children and make families - regardless of your opinion or mine. Ultimately, those who choose a different lifestyle are well within their right to do so. The journey of parenting such a young person can be a long one. You may very well be older or in heaven before they really begin to turn the tide in their struggle. But the job description of a parent never changes. You are never to be *outcome dependent* upon your teen's behaviors for your own joy and happiness. If your child gets help with their issues and their journey brings them back to Christ – wonderful. If your teen takes the other route and begins living a life you never would have planned for them – they are still loved and cared for by our amazing God. He will pursue them. This journey may not always travel through personal happiness but it does lead home. Jesus has risen. You can trust Him.

Appendix

1. Rethinking the Parenting Role

Many times we take parenting as our own[11]. We forget the call to incarnate the love of Christ. When this happens our parenting can easily become governed by *our* wants, *our* desires, *our* comfort and *our* pleasure. Much of our anger can center on the fact that we become *relationship thieves*. We must remember that people don't belong to us, not even our kids - they belong to God. Relationships (such as parenting) are not primarily for our fulfillment. And parenting is often messy, demanding, and labor intensive. Never forget that through relationships, (including parenting a gay or trans child) God gives us opportunity to serve troubled, hurting and confused people everyday. It's a vital role in the kingdom of God.

1. Where is Christ's love missing in your parenting? The way you speak? Think? Act?

2. In what ways can you serve your troubled or hurting teen?

3. What does God expect of you as the parent of a child with SSA or trans confusion? How do you know what He expects?

2. Anger in parenting

1. Do I get angry at the right things?

- Is it righteous anger?
- Selfish anger wants all of God's power with none of God's character. It's 'might makes right' thinking.
- Am I angry because my child is struggling with this?
- Do I have a distorted view of what should make me angry?
- Example of Jonah chapter 4.
- Anger always reveals my heart and what I love most.
- Anger is not to be used to bully your child into obedience.

3. How to pray for your confused teen

- Pray for _redemptive turmoil_ to surround them. Pray that your teen will never find peace, joy or contentment outside of God's will for them. Pray for physical safety and spiritual discontent. As the prodigal sensed his spiritual need so would they.
- Pray that they would foster healthy, growing relationships with Christian heterosexual friends – that gay or trans friendships wouldn't be their only source.
- Pray that they would desire Christ above their own wants. That they would learn to die to self and truly come alive in the Lord.
- Pray that their identity would never firmly root in their orientation but that they would, over time, find their identity fully and completely in Christ.
- God knows the beginning from the end. Pray for your own sanity and patience as you shepherd your teen through this season.

Notes / Thoughts / Action plan

Suggested Resources

1. CCEF (Christian Counseling and Education Foundation)
   * Website has helpful booklets and resources.
   * Training for counselors and helpers.
   * Resources (some free) from a Christian worldview.
2. *When People are Big and God is Small*, Ed Welch
   * How to avoid parenting from fear and anger.
   * How to focus on loving more and needing less.
   * Surviving intact no matter what others do.
3. *Idols of the Heart*, Elyse Fitzpatrick
   * Checking your heart for idolatrous relationships.
   * How to know if you have made an idol of your child's behavior.
   * Refocusing your inner man / woman on the Lord.
4. PFOX (Parents and Friends of Ex-Gays)
   * Testimonies from former Gay and Lesbian people.
   * Video stories of real change in real lives.
   * Resource of hope for change in those that desire it.
5. Focus on the Family
   * Decades old ministry to the family.
   * Conservative evangelical in nature and teaching.
   * Hundreds of resources on parenting in tough situations.
6. *Depression, A Stubborn Darkness*, Ed Welch
   * Gives great understanding to the clinical and spiritual sides of depression.
   * Compassionate, practical help for people in the struggle.
7. *Sacred Parenting*, Gary Thomas
   * Understanding how our kids change and impact us spiritually.
   * Helps with the bigger picture of the parenting role.
   * Promotes parenting from a Christian worldview.

Endnotes

[1] www.healthyplace.com article published 2016 *"Homosexuality and Suicide."*

[2] According to recent Gallup polls.

3. Dr. Paul R. McHugh, John's Hopkins University among many other credible sources. The human genome project also shed much light on the search for the non-existent gene.

[4] The official stance of the American Psychological Association (APA) is in line with this view. According to the APA, "There is no consensus among scientists about the exact reasons that an individual develops a heterosexual, bisexual, gay, or lesbian orientation. Although much research has examined the possible genetic, hormonal, developmental, social, and cultural influences on sexual orientation, no findings have emerged that permit scientists to conclude that sexual orientation is determined by any particular factor or factors. Many think that nature and nurture both play complex roles; most people experience little or no sense of choice about their sexual orientation" (American Psychological Association, 2008, p. 2).

[5] According to the American College of Pediatricians, article dated 2010.

[6] APA.org article from 2015, applauding then president Obama's call to end such therapies.

[7] As of this writing, both California and New Jersey have laws in effect that prohibit any type of change therapy or reparative therapy. Others are sure to follow.

[8] Ed Welch, When People are Big and God is Small, pg. 183.

[9] This is not just an SSA issue. Many people react in heterosexual sin in response to trauma. The young lady who suffers abuse and tormented with bullying may become promiscuous in an attempt to deal with the inner conflict. Just one scenario of many.

[10] Special thanks to Kinshiro Shimochi for this section.

[11] Adapted and modified from Tripp, *Instruments in the Redeemer's Hands,* 120.

Made in United States
Orlando, FL
02 June 2022

18407428R00015